W9-DFI-289

523.4
Asi

ISAAC ASIMOV'S NEW LIBRARY OF THE UNIVERSE

THE RINGED PLANET: SATURN

96-9886

BY ISAAC ASIMOV
WITH REVISIONS AND UPDATING BY FRANCIS REDDY

OUR LADY OF PERPETUAL HELP SCHOOL
4801 Ilchester Road
Ellicott City, MD 21043

Gareth Stevens Publishing
MILWAUKEE

For a free color catalog describing Gareth Stevens' list of high-quality books, call 1-800-542-2595 (USA) or 1-800-461-9120 (Canada). Gareth Stevens' Fax: (414) 225-0377.

The reproduction rights to all photographs and illustrations in this book are controlled by the individuals or institutions credited on page 32 and may not be reproduced without their permission.

Library of Congress Cataloging-in-Publication Data

Asimov, Isaac.
　The ringed planet: Saturn / by Isaac Asimov; with revisions and updating by Francis Reddy.
　　p. cm. — (Isaac Asimov's New library of the universe)
　Includes index.
　Rev. ed. of: Saturn: the ringed beauty. 1989.
　ISBN 0-8368-1223-9
　1. Saturn (Planet)—Juvenile literature. [1. Saturn (Planet).]
I. Reddy, Francis, 1959-. II. Asimov, Isaac. Saturn: the ringed beauty. III. Title. IV. Series: Asimov, Isaac. New library of the universe.
QB671.A83　1995
523.4'6—dc20　　　　　　　　　　　95-7879

This edition first published in 1995 by
Gareth Stevens Publishing
1555 North RiverCenter Drive, Suite 201
Milwaukee, Wisconsin 53212, USA

Revised and updated edition © 1995 by Gareth Stevens, Inc.
Original edition published in 1989 by Gareth Stevens, Inc. under the title *Saturn: The Ringed Beauty.* Text © 1995 by Nightfall, Inc.
End matter and revisions © 1995 by Gareth Stevens, Inc.

All rights to this edition reserved to Gareth Stevens, Inc. No part of this book may be reproduced, stored in a retrieval system, or transmitted in any form or by any means, electronic, mechanical, photocopying, recording, or otherwise without the prior written permission of the publisher except for the inclusion of brief quotations in an acknowledged review.

Series editor: Barbara J. Behm
Design adaptation: Helene Feider
Production director: Teresa Mahsem
Editorial assistant: Diane Laska
Picture research: Kathy Keller and Diane Laska

Printed in the United States of America

1 2 3 4 5 6 7 8 9 99 98 97 96 95

To bring this classic of young people's information up to date, the editors at Gareth Stevens Publishing have selected two noted science authors, Greg Walz-Chojnacki and Francis Reddy. Walz-Chojnacki and Reddy coauthored the recent book *Celestial Delights: The Best Astronomical Events Through 2001.*

Walz-Chojnacki is also the author of the book *Comet: The Story Behind Halley's Comet* and various articles about the space program. He was an editor of *Odyssey,* an astronomy and space technology magazine for young people, for eleven years.

Reddy is the author of nine books, including *Halley's Comet, Children's Atlas of the Universe, Children's Atlas of Earth Through Time,* and *Children's Atlas of Native Americans,* plus numerous articles. He was an editor of *Astronomy* magazine for several years.

CONTENTS

We live in an enormously large place – the Universe. It's just in the last fifty-five years or so that we've found out how large it probably is. It's only natural that we would want to understand the place in which we live, so scientists have developed instruments – such as radio telescopes, satellites, probes, and many more – that have told us far more about the Universe than could possibly be imagined.

We have seen planets up close. We have learned about quasars and pulsars, black holes, and supernovas. We have gathered amazing data about how the Universe may have come into being and how it may end. Nothing could be more astonishing.

Within our own Solar System is a world that many think is the most beautiful object in the sky. It is the giant planet Saturn, with its spectacular rings and numerous moons. Nothing else we can see in the heavens is quite like Saturn. Once you look at it, it is hard to tear your eyes away.

Isaac Asimov

Saturn's Mysterious Ears

In 1610, an Italian astronomer, Galileo Galilei, became the first person to view Saturn through a telescope. Saturn was the farthest known planet at the time. Galileo saw what appeared to be "ears" on each side of the planet that would disappear from time to time!

A Dutch astronomer, Christian Huygens, made use of a better telescope by 1655. Huygens saw that Saturn's "ears" were actually rings encircling the planet. As Saturn orbited the Sun, Huygens saw the rings at different angles. When he saw the rings from the side, they were so thin they seemed to disappear. That was why Galileo, whose telescope was not as good, thought the rings sometimes disappeared.

! The legend of the disappearing ears

Saturn brings to mind a story about an ancient god the Greeks called Cronus. It was believed that Cronus once ruled the Universe. He was afraid his children would take over his job. So each time a child was born to him, he swallowed the child. But his wife was able to save one child. When this child grew up, he did indeed take Cronus's place. When Galileo saw Saturn's "ears" disappear, legend has it that he said, "What! Does Saturn still devour his children?"

Top and opposite: Galileo did not invent the telescope, but he was the first to use it for astronomy.

Bottom: Christian Huygens improved the telescope. He could see that Saturn's "ears" were really rings.

Opposite, inset: Galileo's early sketches of Saturn.

The Second Largest Planet

Saturn is the second largest planet in our Solar System. It is about 75,000 miles (120,000 kilometers) across. This is about 9 1/2 times Earth's diameter. Saturn is about 1/3 as massive as Jupiter and 95 times as massive as Earth. It is farther from the Sun than Jupiter, located about 886,000,000 miles (1,426,000,000 km) from the Sun. That is 9 1/2 times as far from the Sun as Earth is.

The length of one day on Saturn is under eleven hours. It takes Saturn about 29 1/2 Earth years to make one orbit around the Sun.

Left: This picture shows how Earth would compare if it could be magically placed next to Jupiter and Saturn. You can see why Jupiter and Saturn are known as the "giant planets."

Below: This photograph, returned by a space probe approaching Saturn, shows the planet's bulging middle.

! *Saturn versus Earth– the battle of the bulges!*

Although Saturn is much larger than Earth, it turns much more quickly on its axis – once about every 10 1/2 hours. Its middle regions thus bulge outward at the planet's equator. Earth also has a bulge, but it is much smaller. Earth is only about 13 miles (20.8 km) wider at its equator than at its poles. But Saturn is about 7,500 miles (12,000 km) wider at its equator than at its poles. So Saturn actually looks flattened when you look at it through a telescope!

The Only Planet that Floats!

If Saturn were hollow, you could pack 833 Earths into it. But Saturn has the mass of only 95 Earths. This means Saturn must be made up of very light materials.

One cubic foot of Saturn's material would weigh, on the average, about 44 pounds (19.8 kilograms). This is only about 70 percent as much as a cubic foot of water would weigh. That means Saturn would float on water. If you could imagine putting Saturn on a vast ocean, it would float! As far as scientists know, Saturn is the only world that is lighter than water.

Below: If there were an ocean big enough to put it in, you would see that Saturn could float!

Right: Unlike Earth, Saturn has no rocky surface. It has a deep gaseous atmosphere and a very small core.

hydrogen (93%) and helium (7%)

liquid hydrogen

metallic hydrogen
and helium

core

The Deep Atmosphere of Saturn

The most common substances in the Universe are the two light gases, hydrogen and helium. Saturn is made up mostly of these gases. That is why the planet is so light.

When Saturn is observed through a telescope, nothing on the planet is solid. There is just a thick, deep atmosphere. This atmosphere contains small amounts of certain substances besides hydrogen and helium. These other substances form clouds of many colors. These clouds are the "surface" that is observed when Saturn is viewed through a telescope. Underneath the deep atmosphere, there might be a small, solid core of rock and metal.

Below, left: The Hubble Space Telescope tracked an enormous storm near Saturn's equator in 1994.

Below, right: A close-up shows twisted storm clouds and white cloud spots on Saturn.

Opposite: Saturn's rings arc across a sky thick with clouds. The sunlit rings seem to disappear into Saturn's shadow.

❓ *Saturn – a lightweight giant?*

The four "giant" planets are Jupiter, Saturn, Uranus, and Neptune. Jupiter, Uranus, and Neptune all have densities 1.2 to 1.7 times that of water. Only Saturn has a density less than that of water (0.7 – or 70 percent – of that of water).

Why is its density only about half that of the other giants? We can say that Saturn has more hydrogen and helium than the others, but that does not answer the basic question of "why."

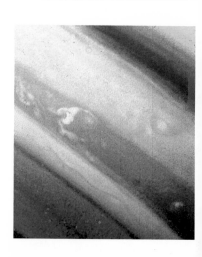

The Ringed Beauty

Saturn is surrounded by rings that circle its equator. The rings are wide, but very thin. The brightest parts are about 45,000 miles (72,000 km) wide, but only about 500 feet (150 meters) thick. This is why the rings seem to disappear when they are observed sideways.

Saturn has two chief rings. These are separated by a space that was first noticed by the astronomer Giovanni Cassini. This space is now called the Cassini Division. Outside the Cassini Division is the *A* ring. On the inner side, closer to Saturn itself, is the *B* ring. Astronomers have identified several dimmer rings outside and inside these two main rings.

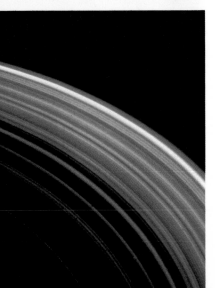

Top: Only a space probe could give us this view of Saturn and its spectacular ring system!

Bottom, left: Scientists colored this *Voyager* photo to bring out hard-to-see details in Saturn's many rings.

Bottom, center: Saturn, its rings, and its moons – Tethys and Dione. The gap in the rings is the Cassini Division.

Bottom, right: The bright areas in this ring contain more matter than the dark areas.

? *The planetary ring club – why is Saturn so different?*

Since 1977, scientists have known that besides Saturn, the planets Jupiter, Uranus, and Neptune also have ring systems. Although Saturn is not the only ringed planet, its rings are the brightest and broadest by far. Why? One theory is that Saturn's ring system is newer than the rest. Perhaps the rings formed from the breakup of a satellite that approached Saturn too closely millions of years ago.

A Closer Look

When Saturn's rings are viewed from Earth, they are too far away to show any detail. But the *Voyager* probes, which reached Saturn in 1980 and 1981, allowed a closer look. They have revealed Saturn's rings in far more detail than ever before.

The probes showed that what looked like only a few rings are actually thousands of smaller ringlets close together, with thin gaps between them. Up close, Saturn's rings look like the grooves of a phonograph record.

Some of the gaps have wavy edges, and one of the ringlets is kinked. Some ringlets separate into two or three parts and appear to be braided.

The rings seem to be made up of pieces of ice and rock – some as small as dust grains, and some as large as houses.

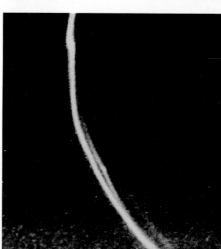

Top: Thousands of ringlets make up Saturn's ring system. One of them, the *F*-ring, is twisted by tiny moons circling nearby.

Center: Dark "spokes" skim over Saturn's rings. The spokes are created by clouds of microscopic particles scattering sunlight.

Bottom: Two tiny moons tug Saturn's *F*-ring into this unusual shape.

Opposite, bottom: Small chunks of ice collide and fragment to form Saturn's magnificent rings.

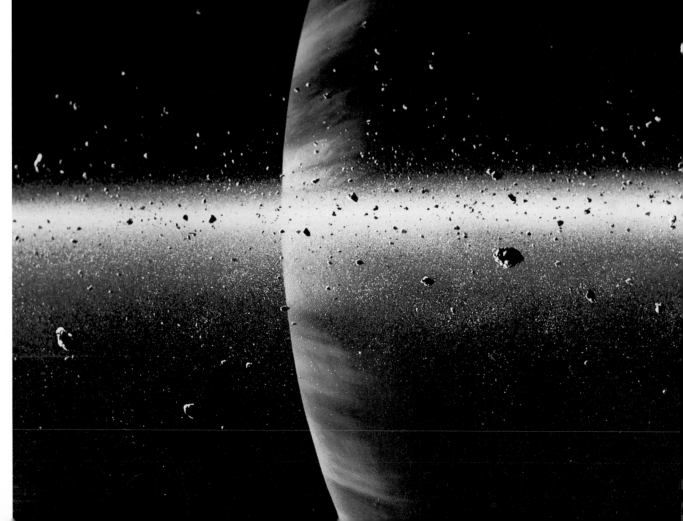

Saturn's Satellite System

Saturn has eighteen confirmed natural satellites, or moons, and astronomers expect to find more.

Eleven of Saturn's moons are at least 120 miles (193 km) in diameter. They were discovered with telescopes from Earth. The others are tiny ones, some only about 11 miles (18 km) in diameter. These were discovered by the *Voyager* probes.

Saturn's moons are spread over a huge distance. The moon nearest Saturn, Pan, is only about 45,500 miles (73,300 km) above Saturn's cloud tops. Saturn's farthest moon, Phoebe, is about 6,540,000 miles (10,521,600 km) away from the planet. That is about 27 1/2 times farther than Earth's Moon is from Earth.

Top: Saturn and its large moons – Dione *(foreground)*, Enceladus and Rhea *(top left)*, Tethys and Mimas *(bottom right)*, and distant Titan *(upper right)*.

Bottom: Who's who in the Saturn system? This painting and its key *(below)* show the orbits of Saturn's larger moons.

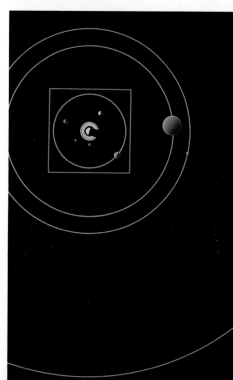

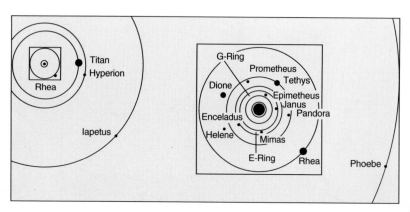

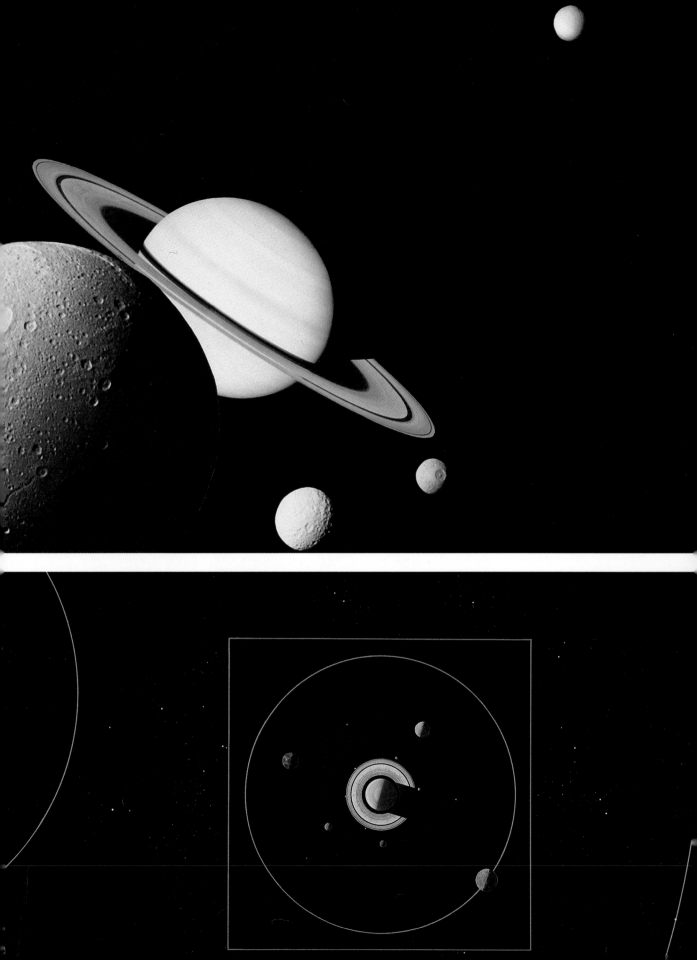

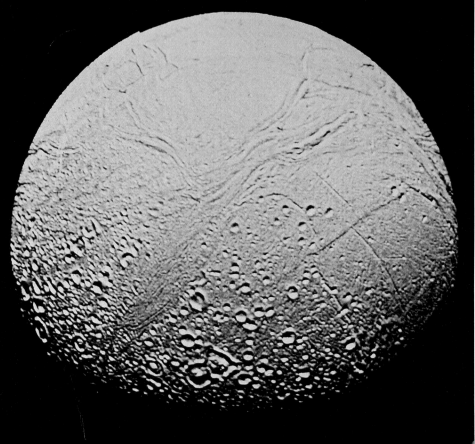

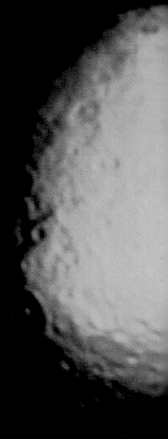

A Mixture of Moons

Saturn's moons come in many different varieties. Enceladus, for example, is about 310 miles (500 km) across. With its gleaming surface, this ball of ice looks as if it were a giant billiard ball!

Iapetus, on the other hand, is about 900 miles (1,440 km) in diameter. It is the second farthest of Saturn's known moons. Iapetus might also be a ball of ice, but it is a dirty one. Iapetus's front side, as it moves around Saturn, is dark, as if covered by dirt. But its rear side is white and shiny. It is a two-toned satellite, but astronomers still don't know why this is so.

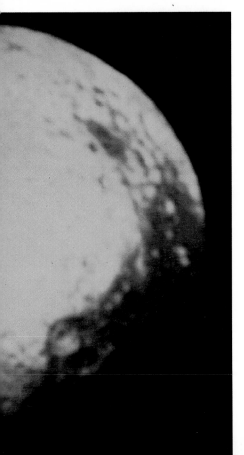

! Saturn's backward moon

The most distant of Saturn's moons – Phoebe – is unusual. It takes about a year and a half to orbit Saturn, but only nine hours to spin once around on its own axis. Phoebe is three times as far away from Saturn as Iapetus, *Saturn's second most distant moon. What's more, Phoebe orbits Saturn in the direction opposite all the other moons. Why is Phoebe so different? Astronomers think Phoebe is not an original moon, but a captured comet or asteroid.*

Top: Something covers up the ice on half of Iapetus, but no one knows what. This painting shows what it might look like where this moon's light and dark sides meet.

Bottom, left: This highly detailed picture of Enceladus was taken by *Voyager 2* from 74,000 miles (119,000 km) away.

Bottom, right: Iapetus as seen by *Voyager 1.*

19

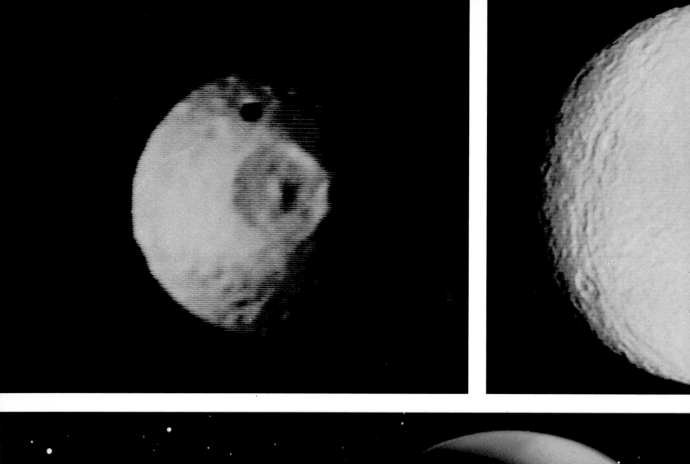

Cratered Worlds

The worlds of our Solar System formed when small pieces of matter all smashed together. Some worlds still have craters – the marks of the final pieces that struck them.

One of Saturn's moons, Tethys, is about 650 miles (1,040 km) across and has a crater 250 miles (400 km) across. Tethys also has a big crack that stretches about two-thirds the way around its surface.

Another moon of Saturn, Mimas, is 240 miles (about 386 km) across. It has a deep, round crater about a third as wide as Mimas itself. Astronomers think the fragment that hit Mimas almost shattered the moon into bits. It was lucky to survive!

Top, left: Little Mimas has a big crater. Mimas may be small, but it's responsible for the Cassini Division in Saturn's rings. The gravity of Mimas sweeps tiny moonlets out of that region.

Top, right: A crack runs two-thirds of the way around the moon, Tethys. Craters large and small pepper the face of this moon of Saturn.

Bottom: Saturn rises over the rugged terrain of its moon Rhea. The largest craters on Rhea were made long ago when the moon collided with leftover fragments of ice and rock orbiting Saturn.

Shepherd Satellites

There are five moons fairly close to Saturn, with diameters between 20 miles (32 km) and 60 miles (97 km). The moons are inside or near the rings. Some of them are given the name *shepherds* because their gravity "herds" the ice grains and boulders that make up the rings, keeping them from drifting too far away and spreading apart. These shepherds keep Saturn's rings compact and bright.

There are at least two tiny moons, each about 11 miles (18 km) in diameter, that move in the orbit of Tethys. One moves ahead of Tethys, and the other stays behind it.

Another moon of Saturn, Dione, has a smaller companion moon called Helene that moves in Dione's orbit. Tethys and Dione are the only moons of Saturn known to share an orbit with other moons.

？ *Did Saturn lose a satellite?*

In 1977, an astronomer named Charles Kowal discovered a distant asteroid that was much farther out in space than any other known asteroid. He named it Chiron. It has an elliptical, or flattened, orbit. At one end, it is a little closer to the Sun than Saturn ever gets. At the other end, Chiron is twice as far as Saturn is. What is an asteroid doing so far out? Maybe Chiron isn't an asteroid at all. Could it have been a satellite of Saturn that somehow got away?

Above: Small moons nicknamed *shepherds* orbit near or within Saturn's rings. Their weak gravity tugs and nudges the tiny ice particles in the rings, sometimes arranging them into unusual patterns.

Left: Saturn's moon Dione has a companion that plays tag. The companion, Helene *(pictured),* orbits Saturn at the same distance from Saturn as Dione. But Helene's distance from Dione changes, moving closer and then farther away.

The Giant Titan

By far, the largest of Saturn's natural satellites, or moons, is Titan. With a diameter of about 3,200 miles (5,120 km), it is the second largest moon we know. Jupiter's moon Ganymede is a bit larger.

Titan is the only known moon that has a thick atmosphere. Its atmosphere is half again as thick as Earth's, and both are mostly made of nitrogen. Unlike Earth, Titan's atmosphere contains a lot of methane. Sunlight breaks up the methane high above the moon, forming chemicals that create a thick haze – and perhaps even rain.

OUR LADY OF PERPETUAL HELP SCHOOL
4801 Ilchester Road
Ellicott City, MD 21043

Far left: Chemicals, such as ethane and acetylene, create smoggy conditions on Titan.

Left: The Hubble Space Telescope was used to construct this crude map of Titan's surface in 1994.

Below: This is the clearest view *Voyager*'s cameras could provide of Titan.

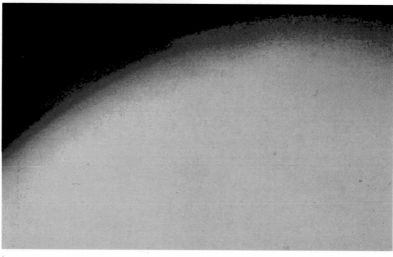

The Voyage of *Cassini*

Astronomers are curious about Titan's surface. The methane in Titan's atmosphere could, under the action of sunlight, form large molecules of tar. On Titan's solid surface of rock and ice, there might be rivers, lakes, or even oceans of liquid methane. And in these oceans, there might be islands – or even continents – of tarry sludge.

Early in the next century, the *Cassini* mission will journey to Saturn. Unlike the *Voyager* missions, which just raced past the planet, *Cassini* will enter orbit around it. That will give scientists more time and opportunity to study Saturn, its complex rings, and its many moons. *Cassini* will be taking a very close look at Titan. It will carry a radar instrument to map Titan's surface, and it will drop a probe called *Huygens* onto the moon's hazy atmosphere. Stay tuned!

Right: The *Cassini* mission will visit the giant moon Titan during its lengthy study of Saturn.

Opposite: About three weeks before *Cassini* first passes Titan, it will release the *Huygens* probe. *Huygens* will collect information on Titan's atmosphere as it falls toward its surface.

Above: The Sun and its Solar System, *left to right:* Mercury, Venus, Earth, Mars, Jupiter, Saturn, Uranus, Neptune, Pluto.

Right: A close-up of Saturn and an assortment of its many moons.

The Moons of Saturn

Name	Pan	Atlas	Prometheus	Pandora	Epimetheus	Janus
Diameter	12 miles (20 km)	19 miles (30 km)	140 miles (225 km)	120 miles (193 km)	55 miles* (88 km)*	60 miles* (97 km)*
Distance from Saturn's Center	83, 250 miles (134,000 km)	85,300 miles (137,248 km)	86,600 miles (139,339 km)	88,100 miles (141,753 km)	94,075 miles (151,397 km)	94,110 miles (151,447 km)
Name	Mimas	Enceladus	Tethys	Calypso	Telesto	1980 S34 ***
Diameter	240 miles (386 km)	310 miles (500 km)	650 miles (1,040 km)	11 miles** (18 km)**	11 miles** (18 km)**	11 miles** (18 km)**
Distance from Saturn's Center	117,000 miles (188,192 km)	149,230 miles (240,151 km)	184,250 miles (296,513 km)	184,970 miles (297,665 km)	184,970 miles (297,665 km)	204,965 miles (329,845 km)
Name	1981 S10 ***	1981 S11 ***	Helene	Dione	1981 S7 ***	1981 S8 ***
Diameter	11 miles** (18 km)**	11 miles** (18 km)**	100 miles (161 km)	700 miles (1,126 km)	11 miles** (18 km)**	11 miles** (18 km)**
Distance from Saturn's Center	204,965 miles (329,845 km)	220,000 miles (353,980 km)	235,300 miles (378,598 km)	235,500 miles (379,011 km)	235,960 miles (379,724 km)	235,960 miles (379,724 km)
Name	1981 S9 ***	Rhea	Titan	Hyperion	Iapetus	Phoebe
Diameter	11 miles** (18 km)**	950 miles (1,529 km)	3,200 miles (5,120 km)	180 miles (290 km)	900 miles* (1,440 km)*	120 miles (193 km)
Distance from Saturn's Center	289,950 miles (466,610 km)	327,940 miles (527,739 km)	758,870 miles (1,221,227 km)	933,360 miles (1,502,024 km)	2,211,430 miles (3,558,786 km)	6,540,000 mil (10,521,600 k

* Diameter at widest point   ** Estimated diameter   *** Not confirmed

Fact File: Saturn

Saturn is the second largest planet in our Solar System, and the sixth closest to the Sun. A "day" on Saturn lasts only a little more than 10 1/2 hours. Since Saturn is more than 9 1/2 times farther from the Sun than Earth is, it takes Saturn much longer than Earth to orbit the Sun. In fact, a "year" on Saturn takes almost 29 1/2 of our Earth years.

Saturn:
How It Measures Up to Earth

Planet	Diameter	Rotation Period (length of day)	Period of Orbit around Sun (length of year)	Moons	Surface Gravity	Distance from Sun (nearest-farthest)	Least Time It Takes for Light to Travel to Earth
Saturn	74,580 miles (120,020 km)	10 hours, 39 minutes	29.46 years	at least 18	1.19*	839-938 million miles (1.35-1.51 billion km)	1.1 hours —
Earth	7,927 miles (12,756 km)	23 hours, 56 minutes	365.25 days (1 year)	1	1.0*	91-94 million miles (147-152 million km)	— —

* Multiply your weight by this number to find out how much you would weigh on this planet.

More Books about Saturn

Our Planetary System. Asimov (Gareth Stevens)
Planets. Barrett (Franklin Watts)
The Planets. Couper (Franklin Watts)
Saturn: The Spectacular Planet. Branley (Crowell Jr. Books)
Solar System. Lambert (Franklin Watts)

Videos

Saturn: The Ringed Beauty. (Gareth Stevens)
Astronomy 101: A Beginner's Guide to the Night Sky. (Mazon)

Places to Visit

You can explore Saturn and other parts of the Universe without leaving Earth. Here are some museums and centers where you can find a variety of space exhibits.

Air and Space Museum
Smithsonian Institution
601 Independence Avenue SW
Washington, D.C. 20560

Astrocentre
Royal Ontario Museum
100 Queen's Park
Toronto, Ontario M5S 2C6

Anglo-Australian Observatory
Private Bag
Coonarbariban 2357 Australia

Henry Crown Science Center
Museum of Science and Industry
57th Street and Lake Shore Drive
Chicago, IL 60637

Hayden Planetarium
Museum of Science
Science Park
Boston, MA 02114-1099

Seneca College Planetarium
1750 Finch Avenue East
North York, Ontario M2J 2X5

Places to Write

Here are some places you can write for more information about Saturn. Be sure to state what kind of information you would like. Include your full name and address so they can write back to you.

National Space Society
600 Maryland Avenue SW
Washington, D.C. 20024

Canadian Space Agency
Communications Department
6767 Route de L'Aeroport
Saint Hubert, Quebec J3Y 8Y9

Sydney Observatory
P. O. Box K346
Haymarket 2000 Australia

The Planetary Society
65 North Catalina
Pasadena, CA 91106

Glossary

asteroids: very small "planets" made of rock or metal. There are thousands of asteroids in the Solar System, and they mainly orbit the Sun in large numbers between Mars and Jupiter. Some also show up elsewhere in the Solar System – some as meteoroids and some possibly as "captured" moons of planets such as Mars.

atmosphere: the gases surrounding a planet, star, or moon.

Cassini Division: the space between the two major rings of Saturn. It is named for Giovanni Cassini, the Italian scientist who first saw this space.

crater: a hole in a surface caused by a meteor strike or volcanic explosion.

diameter: the length of a straight line through the exact center of a circle or sphere. Saturn has a diameter of about 75,000 miles (120,000 km).

equator: an imaginary line around the middle of a planet that is always an equal distance from the two poles of the planet. The equator divides the planet into two half-spheres, or hemispheres.

Galileo: an Italian scientist who, in 1610, became the first to see Saturn through a telescope.

gravity: the force that causes objects like the Sun and its planets to be attracted to one another.

helium and hydrogen: two light gases that are the most common substances in the Universe.

Huygens, Christian: the Dutch astronomer who, in 1655, first identified Saturn's rings.

mass: a quantity, or amount, of matter.

matter: a particular kind of substance or the material that makes up an object.

molecules: the smallest particles of a substance.

probe: a craft that travels in space, photographing celestial bodies and even landing on some of them.

radar: radio waves used to detect distant objects and learn their location and speeds.

rings: the bands of ice, rock, and dust particles that circle some planets, including Saturn, at their equators.

satellite: a smaller body, such as a moon, orbiting a larger body, such as a planet.

"shepherd" satellites: small moons, or moonlets, that orbit within or near Saturn's rings. Their weak gravity helps keep ring matter from drifting out of position.

Solar System: the Sun, planets, and all the other bodies that orbit the Sun.

Index

Born in 1920, Isaac Asimov came to the United States as a young boy from his native Russia. As a young man, he was a student of biochemistry. In time, he became one of the most productive writers the world has ever known. His books cover a spectrum of topics, including science, history, language theory, fantasy, and science fiction. His brilliant imagination gained him the respect and admiration of adults and children alike. Sadly, Isaac Asimov died shortly after the publication of the first edition of *Isaac Asimov's Library of the Universe.*

The publishers wish to thank the following for permission to reproduce copyright material: front cover, © George Peirson 1988; 4 (upper), British Museum; 4 (lower), AIP Niels Bohr Library; 5 (large), The Granger Collection, New York; 5 (inset); Laurie Shock/© Gareth Stevens, Inc. 1988; 6-7, NASA; 7, Jet Propulsion Laboratory; 8, © Tom Miller 1988; 8-9, © Lynette Cook 1988; 10 (left), Reta Beebe (New Mexico State University), D. Gilmore, L. Bergeron (STScI), and NASA; 10 (right), Jet Propulsion Laboratory; 11, © John Foster 1988; 12 (left), Jet Propulsion Laboratory; 12 (right), 12-13 (both), NASA; 14 (both), Jet Propulsion Laboratory; 14-15, © Larry Ortiz 1988; 15, NASA; 16, Laurie Shock/© Gareth Stevens, Inc. 1988; 16-17 (upper), NASA; 16-17 (lower), © George Peirson and Debra Peirson 1988; 18, NASA; 18-19 (upper), © Michael Carroll; 18-19 (lower), NASA; 20, Jet Propulsion Laboratory; 20-21 (upper), NASA; 20-21 (lower), © Joe Tucciarone; 22-23 (upper), © Julian Baum 1988; 22-23 (lower), NASA; 24-25, © George Peirson 1988; 25 (upper), Peter H. Smith of the University of Arizona Lunar and Planetary Laboratory, and NASA; 25 (lower), NASA; 26, 27, © Michael Carroll; 28, © Sally Bensusen 1988; 28-29, © Sally Bensusen 1987.